Fantastic Shrink Plastic

Jewellery & Crafts

Natalia Colman

A note to readers

When working with shrink plastic and other suggested products and tools, readers are strongly cautioned to follow the manufacturers' instructions and warnings. The techniques and materials described in this book are aimed at adults. Children should be carefully supervised by an adult if making any of the projects in this book.

All photography by David Airey unless otherwise noted.

Colman, Natalia
Fantastic Shrink Plastic: Jewellery & Crafts

Interior design & typesetting: Pantek Media
Produced by: Natalia Colman

Printed and bound in the UK by Ashford Colour Press, Gosport, Hants

First printing: 2012

ISBN: 978-0-9570968-2-0

CONTENTS

ACKNOWLEDGMENTS

I love jewellery. There, I've confessed and feel so much better for it. I love everything about wearing it, looking at it, designing it, making it and admiring other people wearing it too! I sometimes have to pinch myself that I have such a terrific job, where I get the time and space to make, create and design jewellery and to think about it all day long. In buying this book, you have given me the opportunity to continue doing what I love and I thank you for this from the bottom of my heart.

I wouldn't have been able to bring you this book without the dedication and talent of David Airey. He is a fabulous photographer who works tirelessly to capture every image and enhances each piece with his skill and patience. Thank you David for your care and attention to detail and for being such a joy to work with.

Thank you to Jo Constable at Pantek Media who created the beautiful graphic design for this book. Jo, you are a genius!

Finally, I want to say a special thank you to Beads Direct and in particular to John Leach, Claire Humpherson and Vicki Downes for all your help and support with this book. It is a real pleasure and privilege to work with you.

Best wishes,

Natalia

INTRODUCTION

The Wonderful World of Shrink Plastic

Since the very moment I started to experiment with shrink plastic I've found that not only does it produce beautiful crafts and jewellery, the process of creating these pieces is extremely rewarding. I'm very creative but not naturally artistic, yet through the drawing and colouring aspects of decorating shrink plastic I've unleashed my inner artist.

Working with shrink plastic is incredibly enjoyable and it is a very cost effective hobby. The beauty of this wonderful medium is that you never really know how it will look until you have baked or shrunk your design, so you get a lovely surprise every time.

I hope you find the information and techniques in this book give you the confidence to create your own beautiful projects. Don't forget to experiment, use your imagination and most of all have great fun. Welcome to the wonderful world of shrink plastic!

SHRINK PLASTIC ESSENTIALS

What is shrink plastic?

It is said that shrink plastic was originally invented by two house wives from Wisconsin, USA, who accidentally shrunk the plastic top of a delicatessen container and discovered this could be turned into a form of craft. I remember doing the same experiments myself as a child with my friends, shrinking crisp packets in the oven and turning them into cute little miniatures to put on key rings.

Today we have the luxury of using sheets of shrink plastic which are thin, flexible polystyrene plastic sheets that shrink when heated in an oven or with a heat gun.

Until recent times, shrink plastic was regarded as a craft for children but this is no longer the case. The wonders of shrink plastic have since been discovered by card makers and scrap bookers. These canny crafters have found that they can decorate a sheet of shrink plastic with coloured pencils and pens, then shrink it down to miniscule proportions to add a very individual and personal little embellishment to their work.

As soon as I laid eyes on shrink plastic my thoughts immediately turned to jewellery and how I could use this medium to adorn necklaces, rings, brooches, earrings and cufflinks. I've found that the possibilities are endless.

Shrink Plastic Products

There are a few different shrink plastic products on the market; the main ones you will come across are Polyshrink, Shrinkles and Shrinky Dinks.

Each manufacturer produces their own sheets in different sizes and colours. Some products can be shrunk in an oven or with a heat gun. Different manufacturers recommend different methods, heat settings and timings. It is important to follow the manufacturer's instructions on each pack, so that once you have created your pieces of artwork, you know how to shrink them and how long to shrink them for.

For ease of explanation of the different methods and techniques in this book, I have used Shrinkles shrink plastic for each project.

Shrinkles Sizes

Shrinkles plain shrink plastic sheets come in two different sizes:

Art sheets (262mm x 202mm)

Craft sheets (130mm x 100mm)

The Art sized sheets are perfect for smaller projects such as rings and earrings. The Craft sized sheets offer a wider range of possibilities to work in a larger scale to make flowers and 3D creations. Since the Art sheets are over twice the size of the Craft sheets, they also represent better value for money.

Shrinkles Colours

Both the Art and Craft sized sheets come in a wide variety of colours. At the time of writing the following colours are available:

- Crystal clear

- Black

- Frosted

- White

- Pastel pink

- Pastel blue

- Pastel yellow

- Pastel green

The frosted and coloured sheets have one side that is shiny and the other side is rough. You can decorate either side of the sheet; however the rough side is easiest to work on as it holds ink and coloured pencils much better.

Crystal clear Shrinkles sheets are completely transparent and are shiny on both sides. These are the only sheets that you cannot decorate with rubber stamp ink or coloured pencils. Glitter gel pens and marker pens work very well on the crystal clear sheets and once your creations have been shrunk, they look like stained glass.

Shrinkles Wallpaper

The Shrinkles brand also offers wallpaper sheets. These are Art sized sheets of shrink plastic that are available in different colours and are pre-printed with six different designs. Wallpaper sheets are an interesting alternative to the blank shrink plastic sheets as you can colour in the pre-printed designs or simply cut out the shape you want and shrink it without having to add any other decorative effects.

My favourite type of shrink plastic to work with is frosted as it offers the most versatility. Frosted shrink plastic sheets are partially transparent, so you can trace your design onto the plastic. When the plastic has been shrunk it has a beautiful, icy appearance with a brushed surface on one side and a shiny surface on the other. After you have shrunk your design, you can also add acrylic paint to the rough side of the piece and the colour will show through beautifully on the shiny side.

GET SHRINKING!

Decorate your shrink plastic sheets using pens, pencils and rubber stamps then cut it to size **before** shrinking it. If you want to add paint or embossing powders to the plastic, only do this after shrinking.

Shrink plastic shrinks approximately seven times its original size and becomes approximately seven times thicker upon shrinking, so it's best to cut any holes before you shrink it down. The plastic becomes incredibly thick and tough once it has shrunk; however, you can pierce a hole into it if you heat the plastic up again. Reheating makes it softer and allows you to make a hole but be warned, this is much harder work than creating a hole before shrinking.

Shrinking in an Oven

Oven baking is by far the simplest method of shrinking as most of us have an oven at our disposal.

Each shrink plastic manufacturer has their own heat and time recommendations, so please read the shrinking instructions on their packaging carefully.

1. Take a baking tray and line it with tin foil. The tin foil prevents the plastic from sticking to your baking tray

2. Place the piece of shrink plastic onto the foil lined tray and put it into a cool oven at the temperature recommended by the shrink plastic manufacturer

3. Leave the piece to shrink for around 5 minutes

4. Remove the tray from the oven. If the piece is not flat when you take it out of the oven, place a flat, heavy object on top whilst the plastic is still warm

5. Be very careful when handling the plastic when it has just come out of the oven as it can easily burn your fingers – ouch!

6. Children, if you are baking shrink plastic pieces always make sure that an adult does this part for you!

Shrinking with a Heat Gun

You can also shrink the plastic using a heat gun. This is the quickest and the most fun way to shrink your pieces as you get to see every second of the magical process.

The first few times you shrink your pieces this way can be a little daunting as the intense heat from the gun means the shrinkage happens very quickly. Don't panic; just enjoy watching the magic happen!

1. Do your shrinking on a heat resistant surface as the heat gun is very hot & can easily scorch or melt your work surface

2. Grip the plastic with a pair of pliers or tweezers and hold the heat gun a few inches away from the plastic as the hot air from the gun can often blow the piece away. Within seconds it will begin to curl up and shrink

3. The plastic may curl up tightly and stick to itself. As you continue to heat it, the plastic should flatten out again as it shrinks. If the plastic does continue to stay stuck together, turn off the heat gun, allow the piece to cool for 5 seconds then gently pull the plastic apart. You should hear it pop as the two sides release themselves. **Be very careful when handling the plastic as it gets extremely hot!**

4. Continue heating the plastic until it is fully shrunk and flattens out. This should take less than 30 seconds. Straight after shrinking, whilst the plastic is still warm you may wish to use a heavy, flat object to flatten the plastic out completely.

5. Children, always make sure that an adult does any shrinking with a heat gun for you!

Creating a Shrink Plastic Ruler

Determining how small or large or piece of jewellery will end up after shrinking can be a little tricky. A great way of making this job easier is to create your own shrink plastic ruler by following these simple steps:

1. Draw around a ruler onto a sheet of shrink plastic

2. Mark out inches or centimeters onto your ruler shape and cut it out

3. Shrink your plastic ruler in an oven or using a heat gun

4. You will now have a miniature, shrink plastic ruler. Measure an original pre-shrunk piece of shrink plastic using a normal ruler, then look at the measurement on your shrink plastic ruler. Your shrink plastic ruler will show you the actual size your piece will shrink to.

ESSENTIAL JEWELLERY MAKING TECHNIQUES

Shrink plastic designs look particularly effective when they are combined with beautiful beads or as an adornment to bracelets, earrings and chains.

If you don't already have a background knowledge of jewellery making techniques, here are a few essential steps that will help you complete the projects within this book.

How to open jump rings

1. Use a pair of round nose or flat nose pliers to grip the jump ring on both sides.

2. Move one of the pliers towards you and the other away from you to open the jump ring. This way you are opening the jump ring outwards rather than pulling it apart. Pulling the jump ring apart will distort its round shape.

3. Once you have separated the jump ring you can slide earring wires, chain, another jump ring or necklace clasp onto your jump ring.

4. Follow the same steps to close the jump ring. Grip both ends with your pliers again. Move the jump ring back into place by wiggling the ends back and forth. You will feel the ends sliding against each other. Your jump ring should be perfectly aligned when it is closed.

How to make a wire loop

1. Thread a bead onto a head pin. Grip the head pin approximately 4mm above the bead with your round nose pliers

2. Bend the head pin to a 90 degree angle by moving your pliers away from you. Use your free hand to bend the tail of the head pin around the nose of your pliers to form a complete loop. You might have to reposition your pliers to do this.

3. Grip the loop with your flat or round nose pliers. Use your free hand and wrap the wire around the neck of the loop until it touches the bead.

4. Use some wire cutters to trim off the excess wire as close to the wrap as possible. Take your flat or chain nose pliers to press down the end of the wire that you've cut to leave a neat finish.

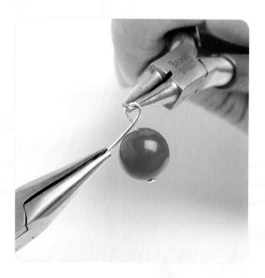

Attaching clasps to a necklace or bracelet

1. Thread a crimp bead onto one end of your beading wire followed by your clasp.

2. Take the end of the wire and fold it back through the crimp bead.

3. Use a pair of crimping pliers or a pair of flat nose pliers to compress the crimp tightly onto the beading thread.

4. Thread the excess beading wire back through two or three beads and trim the excess wire.

5. Follow the same process for the other end of your necklace or bracelet, this time use a jump ring instead of a clasp. You will do this after you have finished stringing your beads onto your necklace or bracelet.

How to create a stretchy bracelet

1. Take some beading elastic and cut off a piece that is twice the length that you need.

2. Thread your shrink plastic creation and beads onto the elastic in the desired pattern.

3. Take the ends of the elastic and tie an overhand knot.

4. Tie a second knot and pull the elastic tightly.

5. Add a drop of clear nail varnish to the knot and allow this to dry. The nail varnish will help to make the knot more secure.

TOOLS & EQUIPMENT

Essential Tools

The good news about making jewellery with shrink plastic is you don't need to invest in lots of expensive equipment and tools.

Here are some of the items that I find very helpful and that I have used to complete the projects in this book.

Heat Gun Tool

It's not essential to have a heat tool but it certainly makes shrinking your plastic pieces quick and easy. It's also incredibly useful for drying the ink or paint on your pieces quickly. In some of the later projects I've used embossing powders on the shrink plastic and these give a really beautiful effect. If you want to add embossing powders to your work then you will need to invest in a heat gun.

Heat Proof Surface

Whenever you are using a heat gun you will need to ensure that you place a heat proof service underneath it to avoid scorching your work surface. I have found that a large tile or firing brick both work well. You could also shrink the plastic on a foil lined baking tray on your stove top.

Domestic Oven

Shrink plastic only needs a low heat for the shrinking to happen, always read the manufacture's instructions on the packaging for precise temperatures and timings. I have also found that a halogen oven does an excellent job of shrinking the plastic.

Scissors

To make each of the projects within this book you will need to cut out various shapes from the shrink plastic sheets. A pair of small sharp scissors work best as you will often have to cut different angles, such as the petals on the flower shapes. The best ways to cut out complex shapes is to cut in one direction first and then to go back and cut in the opposite direction, otherwise the plastic sheets may crack and split.

Single-Hole Punch

A single hole punch is a vital part of your tool kit. In most cases you will need to punch a hole in your shrink plastic so that you can add a jump ring to it once it has been shrunk. The single hole punch creates a hole that is the perfect size for a jump ring or jewellery wire to easily pass through after shrinking. Make sure that you allow at least 5mm between the hole and the edge of the shrink plastic.

Flat Nose Pliers

These are perfect for gripping your piece of plastic as you shrink it with a heat gun. Flat nose pliers are also useful for opening jump rings, wrapping wire and securing crimps when finishing necklaces and bracelets.

Round Nose Pliers

These are essential jewellery making pliers for creating wire loops and opening jump rings.

Black Marker Pen

You will see just how useful a permanent marker pen with black ink can be when you see how many times I use one throughout the different projects. I find that fine point gives good precision when drawing lines and shapes; it is also thick enough for colouring in.

Glitter Gel Pens

Whenever I'm designing or making a piece of shrink plastic jewellery these pens usually are the first things that I pick up. Use the glitter pens to colour the surface of your shrink plastic. When you have shrunk it down, you will see what a beautiful effect it gives. The colour intensifies giving a glorious glittery surface. You can also use the pens after shrinking to add extra sparkle.

Coloured Pencils

When you colour in the surface of the plastic with coloured pencils before shrinking, the result may not look particularly impressive. Do remember that the plastic shrinks seven times smaller and this in turn gives a wonderful intensity to the pencil colours. I love the effects that can be created using coloured pencils. They are more subtle than pens and give the jewellery a water colour look.

Acrylic Paints

Frosted shrink plastic is the most versatile of all the different colours as you can paint it any colour you like. You will achieve the best results by painting the rough side of the shrink plastic after it has been shrunk. One coat of acrylic paint gives the plastic a streaky, colour washed appearance which can look very arty and attractive. Add a second or third coat of paint if you want the colour to be stronger and more even.

Glue

I love to create pieces of jewellery that are three-dimensional, such as the owl pendant. The best way to do this is to cut out the individual pieces, decorate them, shrink them down, and then glue them together. I've found that two-part resin glue works very well. Strong jewellery glues also give a good bond when gluing two pieces of shrink plastic together.

Jewellery Wire

The most secure way of joining two pieces of shrink plastic together is to use some jewellery wire. Silver plated or copper wire is perfect for this purpose. I find that 0.6 or 0.8 gauge works very well and is easy to bend and wrap without breaking too easily.

Cocktail Sticks

These are great for mixing two-part resin glue and applying the glue to your jewellery with greater precision.

Master tools & materials list

Here is a list of all the items I have used to make the projects in this book. If you do other crafts or jewellery making, you may find that you already own some of these tools and materials.

- Craft knife
- Single-hole punch
- Cocktail sticks
- Ink pad
- Rubber stamps
- Scissors
- Pencil
- Coloured pencils (assorted colours)
- Glitter gel pens (assorted colours)
- Black marker pen (fine point)
- Felt-tipped pens (assorted colours)
- Assorted beads
- Jump rings
- Chain
- Jewellery wire (0.6 or 0.8 gauge)
- Beading wire
- Crimp beads
- Necklace clasps
- Earring wires
- Round nose pliers
- Flat nose pliers

- Wire cutters

- Beading elastic

- Clear nail varnish

- Two-part resin glue or jewellery glue

- PVA glue

- Embossing powders

- Acrylic paint (assorted colours)

- Paint brush

- Ribbon

- Flat back crystals

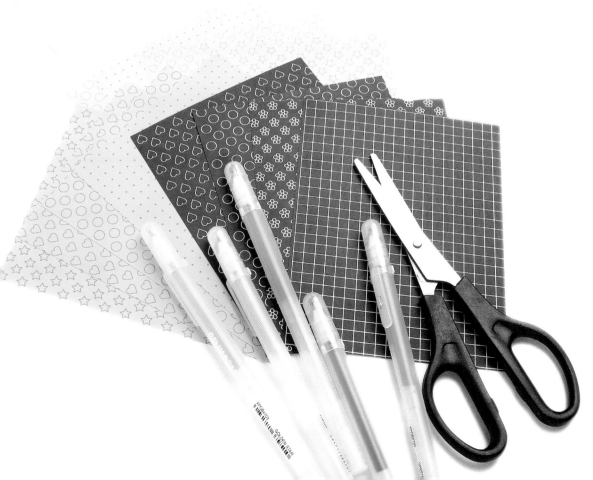

SECTION 1
DECORATING WITH PENS

The humble black marker pen can be the most useful item when decorating shrink plastic for jewellery and crafts. Use one with a fine point so you can get clear lines and markings when drawing onto the shrink plastic sheets. I have found that this type of pen draws easily on the rough or the shiny side of the plastic and when you shrink the plastic down it creates a very elegant, more subtle effect.

Glitter gel pens seem to work like magic on shrink plastic. I have used them to decorate both sides of the plastic throughout the projects in this book. When colouring the shiny side of the plastic, you may need to scribble occasionally with the gel pen you are using on a blank sheet of paper to get the ink flowing. If you are impressed about how glittery your work appears, then wait until you have shrunk it. The finished articles become super sparkly, especially if you decorate the rough side of the plastic.

Felt tipped pens are also ideal for decorating shrink plastic. They work on any colour of the plastic sheets and it's interesting to see how the colours change once the pieces have been shrunk. As the plastic shrinks seven times smaller, the colours you use will intensify and appear more radiant, so you can achieve some wonderful effects.

FOSSIL PENDANT

Fossils have such interesting textures and I wondered how I could incorporate this into a piece of jewellery. Some simple experimenting with tracing the fossil design onto the shrink plastic, led me to create this lovely pendant. I also discovered that some tribal-style beads looked beautiful alongside the rustic fossil design. It is worth experimenting with beads of different sizes and colours to see how they can enhance the shrink plastic jewellery you create.

Materials Needed:

- 1 x craft sized sheet of frosted shrink plastic
- Black marker pen
- 2 x Shepherd hook earring wires
- 2 x 5 mm Jump rings
- 4 x 9 mm Jump rings

1 Take a piece of frosted shrink plastic and trace the design of the fossil template in the Templates section at the back of the book onto the shiny side of the plastic with a black marker pen. Cut out a pendant shape of approximately 18 cm by 13 cm. If you want a smaller sized pendant then cut the plastic to a smaller size. Remember that the plastic shrinks seven times in size, so don't cut it too small.

2 To make matching earrings, cut a rectangular sized piece of frosted shrink plastic about 9 cms by 7 cms in size. Place it in the middle of the fossil template, shiny side up and trace the fossil pattern onto it using a black marker pen. Cut this piece of plastic in half again whichever way looks most flattering for your design.

3 Punch a hole into the pendant and earring designs wherever you would like to place your jump rings when the piece has been shrunk.

4 Shrink the earrings and pendant using a heat gun for a few seconds or by placing all the pieces onto a baking tray lined with tin foil and baking in an oven. Shrink according to the manufacturer's instructions and recommended temperatures.

5 Place a 9 mm jump ring in the hole at the top of the pendant and then add another 9 mm jump ring to this one if the ring is not wide enough for a necklace to go through. Next thread a necklace through the jump ring and your pendant is complete. You may wish to string your pendant onto a necklace with some beads to compliment your design.

6 Place a 9 mm jump ring through the punched hole at the top of each earring. Then add attach a 5 mm jump ring to it and attach the earring wire to the 5 mm jump ring. Your earrings are now complete and you have a beautiful matching jewellery set.

STAINED GLASS-EFFECT EARRINGS

The beauty of frosted and clear shrink plastic is that you can trace a design onto it. Frosted shrink plastic is a favourite of mine because it is transparent, yet has a wonderful frosty appearance. Clear shrink plastic gives a very effective stained glass look to these earrings. Why not experiment with both types to see which one you prefer?

Materials Needed:

- 1 x Art sized sheet of frosted or clear shrink plastic
- Black marker pen
- Glitter gel pens
- 3 x 9 mm Jump rings
- 2 x 5 mm Jump rings
- 2 x Shepherd hook earring wires

1 Take a piece of frosted shrink plastic. Cut the plastic into 2 rectangular pieces measuring 4.5 cms by 8.5 cms.

2 Draw a stained glass design on a piece of blank paper. If you don't want to draw your own design you can always trace over an existing design. Place each shrink plastic rectangle shiny side up on top of your design and trace the it using a black marker pen.

3 Colour in the spaces of the design any way you like using the glitter gel pens. Do leave some parts of the design clear as this gives a lovely effect. You can also use clear shrink plastic, experiment to see the different end results you can come up with.

4 Punch a hole at the top of each shrink plastic rectangle for the jump rings, the plastic is very tough and thick once it has shrunk so remember to do this before you shrink it! Don't worry if you forget, you can always drill a hole when the plastic has shrunk.

5 Shrink the earrings using either a heat gun for a few seconds or by placing all the pieces onto a baking tray lined with tin foil and baking in an oven. Shrink according to the manufacturer's instructions and recommended temperatures.

6 Place a 9 mm jump ring through the punched hole at the top of each earring and then add a 5 mm jump ring to this. Next, attach the earring wires to the 5 mm jump ring. Your earrings are now complete.

ROMANTIC HEARTS

I'm a true romantic, so a heart was one of the first shapes that I created using shrink plastic. These little hearts are so easy to make and you can add the words that are most meaningful to you. My favourite quotation is "*Whatever souls are made of yours and mine are the same*" from Emily Bronte's book, Wuthering Heights and I couldn't resist capturing this within a beautiful heart. Why not create your own 'heart tree' for Valentine's Day? These lovely hearts look perfect tied onto some pieces of curly willow with pretty, colourful ribbons.

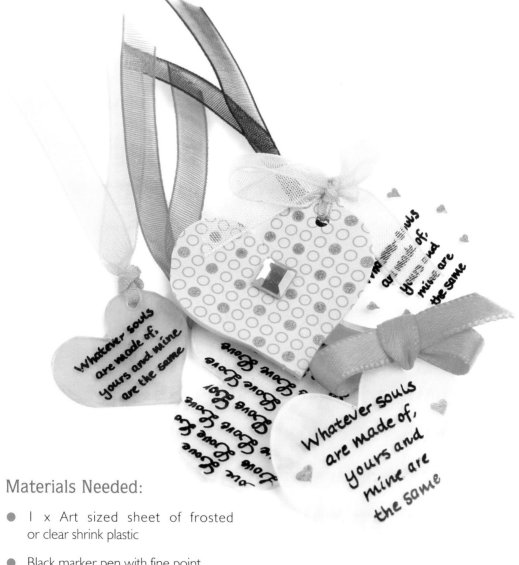

Materials Needed:

- I x Art sized sheet of frosted or clear shrink plastic

- Black marker pen with fine point

- Glitter gel pens

- Colourful ribbons

1 Take a piece of frosted or clear shrink plastic. Use the heart shaped template in the Templates section at the back of the book to draw around onto the shrink plastic sheet. Cut out the heart shape from the plastic.

2 You can write your romantic phrases or words onto the shrink plastic hearts in your own handwriting. If you prefer, create a template of your phrases or words using the font of your choice and print this out from your PC. Place the cut out shrink plastic heart over the wording template and trace over it using a black marker pen.

3 Decorate your shrink plastic hearts with your own designs using the glitter gel pens.

4 Punch a hole at the top of each heart shape, the plastic is very tough and thick once it has shrunk so remember to do this before you shrink it.

5 Shrink the hearts using a heat gun for a few seconds or by placing all the pieces onto a baking tray lined with tin foil and baking in an oven. Shrink according to the manufacturer's instructions and recommended temperatures.

6 Thread a piece of fine ribbon through the hole to create a beautiful keepsake or to add as an embellishment to a card, scrapbook or gift.

TAGS & LABELS

Shrink plastic gives you the perfect opportunity to produce your own personal tags and labels. I helped some children at a local school to display the glass jewellery they had made to sell for a special charity event. Each child designed their own 'Handmade by' tag so that it could be displayed proudly alongside their work. As well as being great fun to design and make, these tags and labels bring a new dimension to any handmade creation. They are also a great way to use up left over shrink plastic.

Materials Needed:

- Assorted strips of shrink plastic
- Black marker pen
- Stardust gel pens
- Assorted ribbons

1 Save up any spare pieces of shrink plastic from other projects to use as tags and sentiments labels.

2 Print out words and sentiments using interesting fonts from your computer. If you're using frosted or clear shrink plastic, you can place the piece of shrink plastic on top of the font you've printed out and trace over it using a coloured pen. Add any other designs to your label and then punch a hole in it for the ribbon to go through.

3 If you're using opaque shrink plastic such as black, white, pink or blue then you can draw freehand onto the plastic. It's best to do this on the shiny side. Use glitter gel pens or felt tip pens to add any other drawings or designs to your label.

4 Punch a hole at the top of each tag so that you can add a piece of ribbon to it once it has been shrunk.

5 Shrink your tags and labels using a heat gun for a few seconds or by placing all the pieces onto a baking tray lined with tin foil and baking in an oven. Shrink according to the manufacturer's instructions and recommended temperatures.

6 Thread a piece of fine ribbon through the hole and tie a knot to secure it in place. You now have a beautiful, personally made tag.

SPARKLY SKULLS

Skull jewellery has become extremely popular in recent years, with designers like Butler & Wilson, Ed Hardy and Alexander McQueen bringing them to the forefront of fashion. Skulls have gone from scary to chic, so I thought I'd include my own glittery and colourful skull creations to inspire you.

Materials Needed:

- 1 x Art sized sheet of frosted shrink plastic for each skull
- Black marker pen
- Glitter gel pens
- 1 Metre fabric coloured chain
- 1 x 9 mm Jump ring per skull

1 Place a piece of frosted shrink plastic on top of the skull template in the Templates section at the back of the book and trace around the skull design with a pencil.

2 Cut out the skull shape and punch a hole at the top of the skull so you can add a jump ring to it once it has been shrunk.

3 Use a glitter gel pen in the colour of your choice to colour in the skull. Do this on the frosted side of the shrink plastic as this helps you achieve a much more glittery effect when the skull is shrunk.

4 Use a black marker pen to colour in the eyes and nose socket of the skull. It is now ready to be shrunk.

5 Shrink your skull using a heat gun for a few seconds or by placing it onto a baking tray lined with tin foil and baking in an oven. Shrink according to the manufacturer's instructions and recommended temperatures.

6 Open a jump ring and thread this through the hole at the top of the skull. Attach the open jump ring to one of the links on the fabric chain and close the jump ring. Repeat this process if you would like to add more than one skull to your fabric chain.

This glittery skull also looks very effective hanging from a rubber necklace!

SECTION 2
RUBBER STAMPING & EMBOSSING

A quick, easy and interesting way to add design and colour to shrink plastic is to use rubber stamps. If you have worked with polymer or metal clays or you already have an interest in card making and scrapbooking, chances are you will already own some fabulous texture plates or rubber stamps. If you have, then it's time to go rummaging through your craft boxes to see what treasures you own and how you can incorporate them into your jewellery making. If not, don't worry, there are a wide range of rubber stamps available in craft shops and on craft websites so you will be spoilt for choice.

Shrink plastic is perfect for embossing onto and adds a new dimension of colour and texture to any jewellery design. I personally love to use gold embossing powder as it adds a touch of pure luxury to any pieces of shrink plastic jewellery. You will need a heat gun to melt the embossing powder and I hope the designs in this section show just what a worthwhile investment this can be.

SPARKLY CUFFLINKS

Rubber stamps work very well on shrink plastic. Stamp them onto the rough side of the plastic and this will give you the perfect template to colour in. These cufflinks become extra sparkly and interesting with the help of the glitter gel pens. Add a pair of cufflink findings to the plastic after it has been shrunk using some two-part resin glue. This type of glue is strong enough to keep both components securely joined together.

Materials Needed:

- 1 x Craft sized sheet of frosted shrink plastic

- Rubber stamp design of your choice

- Glitter gel pens

- 2 x Cufflink backs

- Two-part resin glue

1 Take a rubber stamp with the design of your choice and press it into a black ink pad. Take a piece of frosted shrink plastic and press the rubber stamp down firmly onto the rough side of it. Add more ink to the stamp and press it back down onto the frosted shrink plastic to create two identical cufflink designs.

2 Use glitter gel pens to colour in the spaces between the rubber stamp design.

3 Cut each cufflink design out of the shrink plastic sheet with a pair of scissors. .

4 Shrink the cufflink designs using a heat gun for a few seconds or by placing both pieces into an oven. Shrink according to the manufacturer's instructions and recommended temperatures.

5 Use a metal file to roughen up the cufflink backs and also the back of your shrink plastic cufflink designs. This will key the surface and allows the glue to stick more securely to the metal. Allow the glue to dry overnight before wearing.

6 You can use different coloured ink for your rubber stamps and this looks particularly effective on the coloured sheets of plastic. Why not try gold ink stamped on black shrink plastic as shown here?

POPPY PENDANT

These poppy pendants are the perfect project because they combine so many different techniques in one piece of jewellery. It's very therapeutic to create the beautiful poppy picture, which is drawn with coloured pencils and accented with glitter pens.

If, like me, you aren't artistic, simply trace a design from a picture onto the shrink plastic sheet. The coloured pencils may look a little pale and washed out before shrinking, but don't worry; the colours become very vibrant when the plastic is shrunk. The embossing powder frames the design beautifully and adds a special touch of luxury.

Materials Needed:

- 1 x Craft sized sheet of frosted shrink plastic
- Coloured pencils
- Glitter gel pens
- 1 x 9 mm Jump ring
- Sponge pad
- PVA glue
- Gold embossing powder

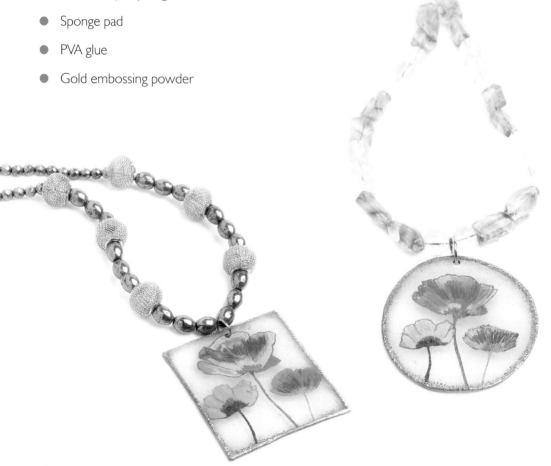

1 Take a sheet of frosted shrink plastic and use coloured pencils to draw and colour your design. If you don't wish to draw your own picture you can trace over an existing design instead.

2 Use the glitter gel pens to add some glittery accents to your design and use a pair of scissors to cut out a circular or square shaped pendant.

3 Use a single hole punch to add a hole at the top of your pendant to suspend a jump ring. Shrink the pendant using a heat gun for a few seconds or by placing both pieces into an oven. Shrink according to the manufacturer's instructions and recommended temperatures.

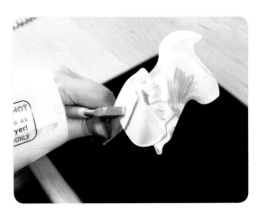

4 Once you have shrunk the pendant, soak a sponge pad with some watered down PVA glue. Press each edge of the pendant into the glue pad to make it sticky.

5 Dip each sticky edge into some gold embossing powder. Use a heat gun to heat the embossing powder until the powder melts and bubbles. Allow the embossed areas to dry and cool for a few minutes. Attach a jump ring and your pendant is complete.

MOROCCAN-STYLE RING & EARRINGS

I was inspired by the colours of Morocco when I made this ring and earrings set. Moroccan colours are always bold and sumptuous and the rubber stamp I used on the plastic reminded me of Moroccan lattice work. The luxurious guilded edge on the flower shapes is created using embossing powders and I added an amazonite cabochon to the centres, for extra colour contrast.

Materials Needed:

- 2 x Art sized sheets of pink shrink plastic
- I sheet of pink Wallpaper shrink plastic with star design
- Rubber Stamp in the design of your choice
- Black ink pad
- Ring mandrel
- Gold embossing powder
- Sponge pad
- PVA glue
- Two-part resin glue
- 3 x Imm Amazonite cabochons
- 2 x 9 mm Jump rings
- 2 x 5 mm Jump rings
- I x Pair of shepherd hook earring wires

1 Take two sheets of pink shrink plastic. Add some black ink to a rubber stamp of your choice and press it down onto one sheet of shrink plastic. Repeat this process for the second sheet of pink shrink plastic.

2 Use the medium flower template in the Templates section to draw a flower shape for the ring onto one of the sheets of stamped shrink plastic. Use the small flower template to cut out two earrings on the other rubber stamped sheet. Punch a hole at the top of each small flower earring before shrinking.

3 Shrink the flower for the ring and the two earring flowers using a heat gun for a few seconds or by placing all the pieces onto a baking tray lined with tin foil and baking in an oven. Shrink according to the manufacturer's instructions and recommended temperatures.

4 After shrinking, whilst the flower shapes are still warm, use your fingers to gently curl up the petal edges. Be careful not to burn your fingers as you do this.

5 Cut a length of wallpaper shrink plastic to make a ring. The long edge of the wallpaper sheet is the perfect size for an open backed ring that is adjustable and fits most finger sizes. Cut the ends into a rounded shape so that the ring is more comfortable to wear.

6 Shrink the ring using a heat tool or by placing it on a baking tray lined with tin foil and baking it in the oven. (Follow the manufacturer's recommended times and temperatures). Once the ring has shrunk, and whilst it is still warm, wrap it around a ring mandrel to create a ring shape.

7 Pour some watered down PVA glue onto a sponge pad. Press the edges of the ring into to sponge to make them sticky.

8 Dip the edges of the ring into some gold embossing powder. Heat the embossing powder using a heat tool until the embossing powder starts to bubble and melt. Allow the embossed areas to dry and cool for a few minutes. Repeat the same process in steps 6 and 7 with the flower earrings.

9 Mix some two-part resin glue. Use a cocktail stick to add a generous amount of glue to the back of one of the cabochons and press this into the centre of the medium flower shape. Repeat this process and glue the two other cabochons to the small flower earrings.

10 Allow the glue on the cabochons to dry for an hour. Mix some more two-part resin glue and use a cocktail stick to place some glue on the front of the ring in the middle. Add some glue to the back of the medium flower and stick it to the ring. Hold the two pieces in place for two minutes then allow this to dry overnight.

11 Attach a 9mm jump ring to one of the flower earrings. Attach a 5mm jump ring to the first jump ring and then add a shepherd hook earring wire. Repeat this process for the second flower earring. Your earrings are now complete.

SECTION 3
MOULDING & SHAPING THE PLASTIC

Just after a piece of shrink plastic has fully shrunk it is very hot and also very flexible. There is a 10 to 20 second window of wonderful opportunity to mould and shape the plastic, to give a more three-dimensional appearance. I first discovered this purely by accident and have since used it time and time again, exploring and experimenting with different methods of moulding and shaping.

Forming with your hands

You can use you hands and fingers to manipulate the warm shrink plastic, be very careful though, as it is very easy to get burnt. Use latex gloves if you can as these can be a very useful barrier in protecting your hands from the heat.

Setting the plastic onto a shape

It's quite easy to mould the warm shrink plastic into a domed shape using a small rubber ball or wooden door knob. The plastic cools down very quickly and sets solidly into whatever shape it is formed into.

Creating Intaglio effects

Finally, I discovered that I was able to create a moulded texture in the warm shrink plastic by pressing down heavily with a rubber stamp. You need very hot plastic and quite a bit of pressure, but the results are quite amazing. This is known as an 'intaglio' effect, this is a process where a design is etched, carved or engraved onto a surface. The rubber stamp creates a wonderful impression on the warm plastic, so it appears to have a carved surface. This technique can be a little hit and miss at first but is well worth persevering with as the results can be quite stunning.

INTAGLIO-EFFECT PENDANT & EARRINGS

It is quite remarkable to see the effects that can be achieved by pressing a rubber stamp into the warm shrink plastic. I love the way that the shrink plastic looks as though it has been carved.

To achieve this effect you need to get the shrink plastic as hot as possible, then press down onto the shiny side with a rubber stamp. You need to apply quite a bit of pressure to achieve a deep impression. It's also best to use a rubber stamp that is mounted on a wooden or Perspex block. If you don't manage to get the effect you wanted, simply heat the shrink plastic up again and the texture you had created will completely disappear as though it has melted away. You can then have another go. It's like magic!

You will get the best results by using pink, blue or black shrink plastic. As you can see with this pedant and earring set, the black plastic looks almost like jet or onyx and retains its super-shiny finish. I used some black onyx cubes and blue agate beads to accompany the pendant. I found that these rainbow haematite rice beads looked particularly beautiful suspended from the shrink plastic.

Materials Needed:

- 1 x Craft sized sheet of black, blue or pink shrink plastic
- Rubber stamp mounted on a wooden or Perspex block
- 2 x Shepherd hook earring wires
- 3 x 9mm Jump rings
- 2 x 5mm Jump rings
- 75cm Length of beading wire
- 5cm Silver plated wire (0.8 gauge)
- 3 x Silver plated head pins
- Beads of your choice
- Necklace clasp
- 2 x Crimp beads

1 Take a piece of black, pink or blue shrink plastic and draw out a template for the shapes of the pieces for your pendant and earrings. I used the lid of an ink pad as this was a perfect size and had attractive, rounded corners. You could also use the lid of a small jar if you prefer to create round pieces for your bracelet and earrings set.

2 Cut out each piece and use a single hole punch to cut a hole at the top and bottom of each one.

3 Shrink each one of the pieces individually using a heat tool. Place the pieces on a heat resistant surface (a glass chopping board or a ceramic tile are both ideal). Hold the heat tool a few inches away from the plastic and within seconds it will begin to curl up and shrink. Don't panic as this is perfectly normal! Keep heating the plastic until it begins to unfurl itself and flatten down.

4 Once the shrinking process has stopped (it takes less than a minute) continue concentrating the heat tool on the piece of shrink plastic until it is very hot and soft. Turn off the heat tool and very quickly, place a rubber stamp on top of the shiny side of the shrink plastic and hold it down, applying as much pressure as possible.

5 When you remove the rubber stamp from the shrink plastic, it should have created a good impression on the shiny side of the shrink plastic, so that it looks carved or moulded. If you didn't put enough pressure onto the rubber stamp, the effect will be quite weak. If you're not happy with it, simply heat up the plastic again for 30 seconds or until the design has disappeared and the plastic becomes soft again and repeat the process.

6 Repeat the process in steps 3 to 5 until you have completed all three pieces. Place a bead onto the end of a head pin. Place the top of the head pin through the hole in one of your shrink plastic pieces. Bend the head pin to a 45 degree angle, then using some round nose pliers, bend the head pin back and wrap the excess wire around the base of the loop. The bead should now be securely attached to the pendant.

7 Repeat the process in step 6 to attach each of the beads that you wish to suspend from the bottom of the earrings and pendant.

8 Attach a 9mm jump ring to the top of a shrink plastic earring. Attach a 5mm jump ring to the first jump ring and then attach a shepherd hook earring wire to the second jump ring. Repeat this process for the second earring.

9 Attach a 9mm jump ring to the hole at the top of the shrink plastic pendant. Thread the pendant onto a length of beading wire and thread on some beads in the design of your choice. Attach a crimp bead and a necklace clasp to each end and trim off any excess beading wire. Your necklace is now complete.

LEOPARD PRINT DOMED EARRINGS

Animal print never seems to be out of fashion, so I could not resist adding a pair of earrings in fabulous leopard print to this collection of shrink plastic jewellery. You can make these in any animal design you wish. I've also made them in zebra, giraffe and pony print. You can find papers with lots of different animal designs in craft shops and on the internet that can be used a template. I used a felt tip pen on frosted shrink plastic to create the leopard print design and added a sparkly accent with a gold glitter gel pen. The colours don't look very strong initially, but once you have shrunk the plastic they intensify and become much more vivid. This was also a great opportunity to show you how to achieve a domed effect with the plastic.

Materials Needed:

- 1 x Craft sized sheet of frosted shrink plastic
- Leopard print paper
- Brown felt tip pen
- Gold glitter gel pen
- Small round lid or bowl (approximately 6 or 7cm diameter)
- Small rubber ball or round object
- 6 x 3mm Beads of your choice
- 2 x Gold plated shepherd hook earrings
- 2 x 9mm Gold plated jump rings
- 2 x Gold plated eye pins

1 Take a sheet of frosted shrink plastic and place it on top of a piece of leopard print paper. Use a brown felt tip pen to copy the design onto the shrink plastic. Add some glittery accents using a gold glitter gel pen.

2 Draw two circles using a small lid or bowl as a template and cut these out.

3 Use a single hole punch to make a hole at the top of each circle shape. This is where you will add a jump ring to suspend your earrings wires when the plastic has been shrunk.

4 Shrink the two circle shapes using a heat gun for a few seconds or by placing both pieces into an oven. Shrink according to the manufacturer's instructions and recommended temperatures.

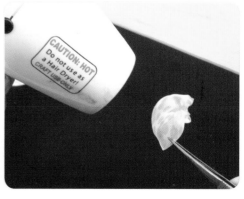

5 Whilst the shrink plastic circles are still warm, place them immediately on a small round object, such as a rubber ball or door knob. Mould the warm plastic onto the round object to give it a domed shape.

6 Allow the plastic to cool before removing it from the round object. If you didn't achieve the shape you wanted, simply heat the plastic up again until it is soft and repeat the process in Step 5.

7 Attach a 9mm jump ring to the hole in one of the shrink plastic dome shapes. Attach an eye pin to this jump ring. Slide 3 beads onto the eye pin. Use the excess wire on the head pin to create a wire wrapped loop at the top of the beads.

8 Open the loop at the base of a shepherd hook earring wire and attach the eye pin to this. Close the earring wire loop to secure the eye pin in place. Your earrings are now complete.

SECTION 4
CREATING
LAYERED PIECES

Creating layers with shrink plastic is where the fun really starts. By creating separate pieces and connecting them together you can achieve some wonderful effects. Some of my favourite designs are here in this section. The 3-D flowers look so beautiful and they are really interesting to make. Experiment by using different colours and cutting out different shapes to form your own flowers. The more layers you create, the more intricate the flower will be. All of the flower petal layers can be joined together very securely by using jewellery or florists wire.

I really enjoy creating nature-themed jewellery, the owl and hummingbird were an absolute delight to design and make. The owl in particular seemed to develop a little personality of his own with every layer!

PEACOCK BROOCH

The first of my three bird projects in shrink plastic, is this lovely little peacock brooch. It was great to see the effect that the green glitter gel pen creates on a piece of black shrink plastic. The black background gives the colour greater density and I managed to achieve a very authentic looking peacock green on the head and neck. A cluster of head pins gives this bird his regal crown and the pearls at the base of his feathers add another interesting dimension to this layered brooch.

Materials Needed:

- I x Craft sized sheet of frosted shrink plastic
- I x Art sized sheet of black shrink plastic
- 6 x Silver head pins
- 3 x 4mm Grey pearls
- Brooch finding
- 4 x Silver head pins
- 30mm Length of beading elastic

1 Take a piece of frosted shrink plastic and use a pencil to trace around the peacock templates in the Templates section onto the rough side of the shrink plastic. Draw the peacock body and eight feather shapes.

2 Take a piece of paper and trace the outline of the peacock's head and neck using the template in the Template section. Cut this shape out then use a pencil to draw around it onto a piece of art sized black shrink plastic. Cut all the pieces out using a pair of scissors.

3 Use a single hole punch to create a hole at the top of the peacock's head. Use a hole punch to cut three, evenly spaced holes at the base of the peacock's body.

4 Decorate the peacock's head by colouring in the beak with a gold glitter gel pen. Colour the head and the neck with a green glitter gel pen.

5 Colour the different peacock feather shapes using the glitter gel pens. Use whichever colours you prefer. I used gold, red, purple, green and silver for my peacock.

6 Shrink the different peacock shapes using a heat gun for a few seconds or by placing all the pieces into an oven. Shrink according to the manufacturer's instructions and recommended temperatures.

7 Mix some two part resin glue and apply some to the top of the peacock's body. Place the base of the peacock's neck on top of the glue and press down. Hold the two pieces in place for two minutes to allow the glue to dry a little and keep the two pieces connected. Allow this to dry fully for three hours.

8 Once the peacock body and neck is fully dry, mix some more two part resin glue and apply this to the back of each feather shape. Place the feather shapes on top of the peacock's body in whatever pattern you wish. Allow this to dry for a further three hours.

9 Push three head pins through the hole at the top of the peacock's head. Allow 1.5 mm of the head pin to protrude from the top of the peacock's head. Gather the excess wires from the head pins together at the back of the peacock and twist them to form one piece of wire. Use some round nose pliers to form a loop, wrap the excess wire around the base of the loop. This will allow you to wear the peacock as a necklace as well as a brooch.

10 Mix some two part resin glue and apply this to the back of a brooch finding. Place the brooch finding on the back of the peacock, at the base of the neck. Hold this in place for two minutes to allow the glue to dry a little. Allow the glued brooch finding to dry fully for three hours and your brooch is complete.

CORSAGE-STYLE FLOWERS

These three-dimensional flowers are so easy to make and look incredibly beautiful when they are complete. You can combine any colour of the shrink plastic sheets, it's worth experimenting just to see what you can come up with and which ones you like best. You can add a brooch to the back our flowers or string them onto a necklace with some pretty beads these flowers would even make a lovely feature for a belt, the choice is yours!

Materials Needed:

- 3 x Craft sized sheets of frosted shrink plastic

- 1 x Sheet of shrink plastic wallpaper

- Glitter gel pens

- Craft knife

- 1 x 6mm pearl

- Half a metre of silver plated wire (0.8 or 0.6 gauge)

1 Take a piece of craft sized shrink plastic and use a pencil to trace the outline of the large flower template in the Templates section onto the rough side of the plastic.

2 Cut the flower shape out using a small pair of scissors. As there are a lot of angles in this design, it is easiest to cut out by cutting in one direction and then cutting in the opposite direction.

3 Trace the outline of the medium and small flower templates onto the rough side of a shrink plastic sheet and cut these out. You can use different coloured shrink plastic sheets or wallpapers for each one.

4 You need to make a hole in the centre of each flower. The single hole punch won't be long to reach the centre, so use a craft knife to pierce a hole in the centre of each one.

5 Shrink the flower shapes using a heat gun for a few seconds or by placing all the pieces into an oven. Shrink according to the manufacturer's instructions and recommended temperatures.

6 Layer the different sized flower pieces on top of each other, starting with the largest flower shape at the bottom and the smallest one on top. Thread a piece of silver plated wire through the holes in the centre of each flower. Thread a pearl onto the wire so that it rests on top of the smallest flower. Snip the wire so that there are just 3 cm of wire protruding from the end of the pearl. Take some round nose pliers and curl the wire around them to create a wire spring. Pull the spring so that it points upwards.

7 Make a loop using your round nose pliers with the wire at the back of the flower. Wrap the excess wire around the base of the loop 3 or 4 times then snip off the excess. Your flower is now complete.

BEADED & LAYERED FLOWER BRACELET

This beautiful flower was created using the same process as the three-dimensional flowers previously but with a twist. I've used frosted shrink plastic and after shrinking it, this time I painted the flower layers to give me some different colour options. Painting the rough side of the frosted shrink works best and gives the plastic a beautiful finish. I have also added a bead cluster to the centre of the flower which gives it an extra dimension and makes it much more flower-like. I knew exactly what beads I wanted to accompany the flower, so I decided to paint the flower petals different shades of ochre to match.

Materials Needed:

- 3 x Craft sized sheets of frosted shrink plastic
- 1 x Sheet of shrink plastic wallpaper
- Craft knife
- Acrylic paint in the colours of your choice
- 7 x 3mm Beads in the colours of your choice
- 7 x Silver plated head pins
- Half a metre of silver plated wire (0.8 or 0.6 gauge)
- 30cm Length of beading elastic

1 Take two pieces of craft sized shrink plastic and use a pencil to trace the outline of the large flower template in the Templates section onto the rough side of the sheets of plastic. You will need to create two large flowers for this project.

2 Cut the flower shapes out using a small pair of scissors. As there are a lot of angles in this design, it is easiest to cut out by cutting in one direction and then cutting in the opposite direction.

3 Trace the outline of the medium and small flower templates onto the rough side of a shrink plastic sheet and cut these out. You can use different coloured shrink plastic sheets or wallpapers for each one.

4 You need to make a hole in the centre of each flower. The single hole punch won't be long to reach the centre, so use a craft knife to pierce a hole in the centre of each one.

5 Shrink the flower shapes using a heat gun for a few seconds or by placing all the pieces into an oven. Shrink according to the manufacturer's instructions and recommended temperatures.

6 Mix some acrylic paint in the colour of your choice. Turn each flower over onto the rough side and paint it with acrylic paint then leave to dry. When the paint has dried turn the flower shape over to look at the shiny side. The first coat of paint creates a streaky effect, this can look quite effective. If you prefer a more dense colour, add another one or two more layers of paint to each flower. Allow the paint to dry between coats.

7 Slide each of the beads onto a separate head pin and gather the head pins together in a cluster. Twist the excess wire a few times to create a stem.

8 Layer the different sized flower pieces on top of each other, starting with the largest flower shape at the bottom and the smallest one on top. Thread the wire stem through the holes in the centre of each flower so that the cluster of beads rests on top of the smallest flower.

9 Make a loop using your round nose pliers with the wire at the back of the flower. Wrap the excess wire around the base of the loop 3 or 4 times then snip off the excess. Your flower is now complete.

10 You can create a stretchy bracelet adding the flower as a beautiful centre-piece. Take a length of beading elastic. Slide on the beads of your choice and the flower. Secure the bracelet by tying a knot in the elastic. Tie a second knot and add a drop of clear nail varnish to keep the knot in place. Leave the bracelet for a few hours before trimming the ends of the elastic close to the knot.

You can create lots of bracelets that look completely different to one another simply by using different flower shapes, paint colours and beads. The flower template for this rounded flower shape can be found in the Templates section in the back of the book.

HUMMINGBIRD PENDANT

Frosted shrink plastic works its magic again with this elegant hummingbird pendant. I'm fascinated by nature and I love to make jewellery inspired by birds and animals.

Hummingbirds are very popular in jewellery design, not only are they so colourful and such a beautiful shape, they also symbolise many different things. Because of its speed, the hummingbird is known as a messenger and stopper of time. It is also a symbol of love, joy, and beauty. The hummingbird is able to fly backwards, teaching us that we can look back on our past. But, this bird also teaches that we must not dwell on our past; we need to move forward. When the hummingbird hovers over flowers while drinking nectar, he teaches us that we should savour each moment, and appreciate the things we love.

Materials Needed:

- 1 x Craft sized sheet of frosted shrink plastic
- 1 x 4mm Flat back crystal
- 7 x 3mm Beads in the colours of your choice
- 4 x 5mm Silver plated jump rings
- 2 x 9mm Silver plated jump rings
- Necklace cord

1 Take a piece of craft sized shrink plastic and use a pencil to trace the outline of the three parts of the hummingbird in the Templates section onto the rough side of the plastic. Cut each piece out carefully with a pair of scissors.

2 Colour in the body of the hummingbird using some coloured pencils. Use some glitter gel pens to add a glittery accent to the body. Colour in the feathered tail using glitter gel pens in the colours of your choice.

3 Colour in the wing of the hummingbird using coloured pencils along the top of the wing and glitter gel pens along the bottom. Use a fine-tipped black marker pen to draw the outline of feathers along the bottom of the wing.

4 Colour in the beak of the hummingbird with a gold or silver glitter gel pen. Use a single hole punch to cut a hole at the top of the wing to attach a jump ring.

5 Shrink the hummingbird shapes using a heat gun for a few seconds or by placing all the pieces into an oven. Shrink according to the manufacturer's instructions and recommended temperatures.

6 Mix some two part resin glue and apply this to the wing and beak and attach these to the hummingbird's body. Hold the pieces in place for two minutes to allow them to set or make sure that they are well supported so that they stay in place.

7 Allow the glued hummingbird to dry for at least three hours. Attach a 5mm jump ring to the wing of the hummingbird. Attach another 5mm jump ring to the first jump ring.

8 Attach a 9mm jump ring to the second jump ring. Slide a necklace cord through the 9mm jump ring and your hummingbird necklace is now complete.

OWL NECKLACE

I have a great love of owls, so it was inevitable that I one of the first projects I created for this book was an owl necklace. There are many aspects of an owl that are so intriguing to look at; therefore this was a piece that definitely needed to be created in layers. It was so much fun to design and I enjoyed finding different components to make my owl as beautiful and life-like as possible. I hope you love making and wearing him as much as I have!

Materials Needed:

- 2 x Craft sized sheets of frosted shrink plastic
- 1 x Art sized sheet of black shrink plastic
- 2 x 1cm Amethyst cabochons
- 3 x 4mm Smokey quartz drop beads
- 2 x 4mm Rainbow haematite rice beads
- 5 x Gold plated head pins
- 1 x 9mm Gold plated jump ring
- ½ metre Fine gold plated chain
- 1 x metre Gold plated chain with large links
- 1 x Gold plated necklace clasp

1 Take a piece of craft sized shrink plastic and use a pencil to trace the outline of the owl's head in the Templates section onto the rough side of the plastic. Take a second sheet of craft sized shrink plastic and use a pencil to trace the outline of the owl's body and beak in the Templates section onto the rough side of the plastic. Cut each piece out carefully with a pair of scissors.

2 Take a piece of paper and trace the outline of the owl's eye using the template in the Templates section. Cut this shape out. Use a pencil to draw around it onto the rough side of an art sized sheet of black shrink plastic. Draw two eyes and cut these out carefully with a pair of scissors.

3 Decorate the owl's body using a fine black marker pen to draw feather shapes and wings. Colour in the body using gold and silver glitter gel pens. Use a single hole punch to cut a hole at the bottom of the owl's body to attach a jump ring.

4 Colour in the beak of owl with a red glitter gel pen. Decorate the owl's head using a fine black marker pen to make a feather effect and colours these in using gold and silver glitter gel pens. Use a singe hole punch to cut a hole at the top of the owl's head to attach a jump ring.

5 Decorate the owl's two eyes by drawing lines radiating out from the centre with a green glitter gel pen. Do this on the rough side of the black shrink plastic as it is easiest to add colour to.

6 Shrink the different owl shapes using a heat gun for a few seconds or by placing all the pieces into an oven. Shrink according to the manufacturer's instructions and recommended temperatures.

7 Mix some two part resin glue and apply this to the back of each of the owl's eyes and his beak. Attach these to the owl's head and allow them to dry for three hours. You may need to hold the pieces in place for two minutes to ensure they stay connected.

8 Mix some more two part resin glue and apply this to the top of the owl's body. Attach the head to this and allow to dry for three hours. You may need to hold the head and body in place for two minutes to ensure the two pieces do not slide apart.

9 Once the owl is fully dry, mix some two part resin glue and apply this to the back of each amethyst cabochon. Stick a cabochon in the centre of each of the owl's eyes. Allow the glue to dry for at least three hours. Hold the cabochons in place for two minutes to allow the glue to set and prevent the cabochons for sliding.

10 Attach a 9 mm jump ring to the bottom of the owl's body. Before you close the jump ring attach five lengths of fine gold plated chain (each one should measure approximately 3 cm in length).

11 Push a gold plated head pin through one of the beads. Use some round nose pliers to make a loop in the head pin and attach it to the bottom of the one of the lengths of fine gold chain. Wrap the excess wire around the base of the loop and trim the excess wire. Repeat this process using the other beads and head pins and attaching these to the remaining lengths of fine gold chain.

12 Attach a jump ring to the top of the owl's head. Attach a length of gold plated chain with large links to the jump ring. Attach a necklace clasp to the two ends of the chain. Your owl necklace is now complete.

PAINTED FLOWER BRACELET

This flower bracelet is made in a similar way to the corsage-style flowers earlier in the book. I wanted to show you how using a different flower shape can create a completely new piece of jewellery. You could add a further layer of petals to the flower if you wish. You could also experiment with painting the flower shapes different colours. I loved the vibrant red of this particular flower and thought it looked perfect teamed with pyrite beads at the centre and crackled agate coins for the bracelet.

Materials Needed:

- 1 x Craft sized sheet of frosted shrink plastic

- Red acrylic paint

- 4 x 3 mm Beads of your choice

- A selection of beads in the colours & sizes of your choice

- 4 x Silver head pins

- 30 mm Length of beading elastic

1 Take a piece of frosted shrink plastic and use a pencil to trace around the flower template in the Templates section onto the rough side of the shrink plastic. Draw two flower shapes.

2 Use a pair of scissors to cut out each flower shape. The flowers are quite fiddly to cut around, you will find it easier to cut down one side and then cut down the opposite side. This avoids tearing the shrink plastic.

3 Make a hole in the centre of each flower before you shrink them, using a craft knife.

4 Shrink the two flower shapes using a heat gun for a few seconds or by placing all the pieces into an oven. Shrink according to the manufacturer's instructions and recommended temperatures. Whilst the shrink plastic is still warm, turn the plastic over so it is shiny side up and gently curl the edges of the petals upwards.

5 Paint the back of each of the flower shapes on the rough side of the shrink plastic with some red acrylic paint, or in the colour of your choice. Allow this to dry. The acrylic paint tends to look a little streaky, so if you would like a stronger colour apply another coat or two of paint. Allow the paint to dry between coats.

6 Place the one flower shape on top of the other so that the hole in the centre lines up. Push a head pin through one of the 3mm beads then push the end of the head pin through the holes in the centre of the flowers. Repeat this process with the other three beads and head pins.

7 Pull the head pins tightly together at the back of the flower and twist until they become one piece of wire. Use some round nose pliers to create a loop in the wire cluster and wrap the excess wire around the base of the loop. Trim off any excess wire.

8 Thread a length of beading elastic through the centre of the wire loop you created on the back of the flower. Thread some beads onto each end of the beading elastic until you have created the desired length to fit your wrist. Tie a knot in the beading elastic. Tie a second knot and trim off any excess beading elastic. Add a drop of clear nail varnish to secure the knot and allow this to dry overnight before wearing.

SECTION 5
JEWELLERY
JUST FOR FUN!

Kitsch and cute jewellery is all the rage, so I have devoted this final section to some very fun and funky pieces for you to enjoy. These are great pieces to make with kids, they will probably come up with far more ideas than I have but here are a few sweet treats to get you started.

Create charms, earrings, pendants and key rings of all your favourite goodies. Use lots of glitter and crystals and have fun wearing and sharing these lovely pieces of jewellery and crafts.

GINGERBREAD PEOPLE
BAG CHARMS

I adore gingerbread people and I could not resist creating this sweet pair to use as bag charms or to adorn a key ring. You can make the gingerbread colour using yellow ochre and red acrylic paint, then jazz up this cute couple with flat back crystals and pearls. They really do make a perfect pair.

Materials Needed:

- 1 x Craft sized sheet of frosted shrink plastic

- 2 x 9mm Silver plated jump rings

- 2 x Silver plated key chain findings

- Assorted flat back crystals & decorative faux pearls

- Yellow ochre acrylic paint

- Red acrylic paint

1 Take a sheet of craft sized frosted shrink plastic and use a pencil to trace the outline of the template for the gingerbread man and woman in the Templates section. Draw your outlines onto the rough side of the shrink plastic.

2 Cut the shapes out using a pair of scissors. Use a single hole punch to make a hole at the top of each shape. Use a fine marker pen or glitter gel pen to draw a mouth on each gingerbread shape on the shiny side of the plastic.

3 Shrink the gingerbread shapes using a heat gun for a few seconds or by placing the pieces into an oven. Shrink according to the manufacturer's instructions and recommended temperatures.

4 Mix some yellow ochre acrylic paint with a tiny amount of red acrylic paint. Keep adding the red to the yellow and mix well until you achieve the desired gingerbread colour.

5 Paint the rough side of the shrink plastic shapes. Allow the first coat of paint to dry and then apply a second coat so that you achieve a strong, consistent colour. Use a heat gun tool to dry each coat of paint quickly. Keep the heat gun at least 15cm away from the gingerbread shape, you want to dry the paint without making the shrink plastic too hot as it will soften again.

6 Once you are happy with the paint colour and it has dried completely, mix some two part resin glue. Use a cocktail stick to apply this to the back of some flat back crystals and faux pearls and stick these to the shiny side of the gingerbread people to decorate them.

7 Attach a jump ring to the hole at the top of one of the gingerbread people. Attach a key chain to the jump ring and close the jump ring. Repeat this process with the second gingerbread person.

8 Your gingerbread couple are now complete. If you like you can also add some colourful beads to the key chain.

FUNKY ZEBRA KEY RING

I was inspired to create this cute zebra when I saw my silver glitter pen and black marker pen lying side by side. He is so much fun to make and always brings smile to my face whenever I look at him. No self respecting bunch of keys should be without a funky zebra key ring!

Materials Needed:

- 1 x Craft sized sheet of frosted shrink plastic
- 1 x Art sized sheet of black shrink plastic
- 1 x 9mm Silver plated jump ring
- 1 x Silver plated key chain finding
- 2 x 4mm flat back crystals
- 2 x 8mm flat back decorative faux pearls

1 Take a sheet of craft sized frosted shrink plastic and use a pencil to trace the outline of the template for the zebra head and two ears in the Templates section. Draw your outlines onto the rough side of the shrink plastic.

2 Cut the shapes out using a pair of scissors. Use a silver glitter gel pen to draw silver stripes onto the zebra's head. Use a black marker pen with a fine tip to colour in the black stripes on his head.

3 Use a fine black marker pen to colour in the edges of the zebra's ears and to draw the outline of his inner ear. Colour the inner ears with a purple glitter gel pen.

4 Take a piece of paper and trace the outline of the zebra's eye, nose and mane using the template on page x. Cut these shapes out, then use a pencil to draw around them onto the rough side of a sheet of black shrink plastic. Cut out all the pieces using a pair of scissors.

5 Colour the top of the zebra's mane with a silver glitter gel pen. Use a single hole punch to cut a hole at the top of the mane for a jump ring.

6 Shrink the different parts of the zebra using a heat gun for a few seconds or by placing the pieces into an oven. Shrink according to the manufacturer's instructions and recommended temperatures.

7 Mix some two part resin glue and use a cocktail stick to apply this to the bottom of the mane and ears. Stick these pieces into place on the back of the zebra's head. Make sure that the pieces are well supported until the glue dries so that they don't slide off.

8 Apply some more two part resin glue to the zebra's nose and the backs of the eyes and stick these in place on top of his face. Use a cocktail stick to apply some glue to the back of two flat back faux pearls and two flat back crystals. Stick these onto the zebra's eyes and nose. Allow the glue to dry for at least three hours.

9 Attach a jump ring to the hole at the top of the zebra's mane and attach a key chain to the jump ring before closing it. Your funky zebra key ring is now complete.

CUTE CUPCAKE KEY RING

Now that cupcakes have become the latest baking phenomena who could resist a sweet little cupcake on their key chain? I found that the glitter gel pens worked like a dream in giving my cupcake just the right amount of sparkle. Use flat back crystals and faux pearls as the sprinkles for extra bling. Beads in matching colours are the perfect accompaniment to give your key chain added style.

Materials Needed:

- I x Craft sized sheet of frosted shrink plastic

- I x 9mm Silver plated jump ring

- I x Silver plated key chain finding

- Assorted flat back crystals or decorative flat back faux pearls

- Assorted beads

- Silver plated head pins

1 Take a sheet of craft sized frosted shrink plastic and use a pencil to trace the outline of the three template shapes for the cupcake in the Templates section. Draw your outlines onto the rough side of the shrink plastic.

2 Cut the shapes out using a pair of scissors. Use a single hole punch to cut a hole for the jump ring at the top right or left hand side of the cupcake.

3 Use a silver or gold glitter gel pen to colour in the cupcake case. Use a fine black marker pen to draw the ribbed lines onto the cupcake case.

4 Colour in the top of the cupcake with a glitter gel pen in the colour of your choice. Colour in the highlight on the cherry shape with a silver glitter gel pen. Colour in the rest of the cherry shape with a red glitter gel pen.

5 Shrink the different parts of the cupcake using a heat gun for a few seconds or by placing the pieces into an oven. Shrink according to the manufacturer's instructions and recommended temperatures.

6 Mix some two part resin glue and use a cocktail stick to apply this to the front of the cupcake case, at the top. Stick the top of the cupcake to the case and hold the two pieces in place for two minutes to allow the glue to dry a little.

7 Apply some more two part resin glue to the back of the cherry and stick this to the top of the cupcake. Allow the glue to dry for at least three hours.

8 Attach a jump ring to the hole at the top of the cupcake and attach a key chain to the jump ring before closing it. Your cute cupcake key ring is now complete.

SWEET TREATS BAG CHARMS

This final project was my opportunity to indulge myself in making all the little sweet treats that I love. These pieces are so bright, colourful and wonderfully cheerful. I added the most pretty and happy looking beads I could find in my bead boxes to accompany the bag charms. I've made these three to inspire you, but why not create your own designs based around the sweet treats that you like most of all? These charms make perfect gifts so why not make these as a treat your friends and family or even as a gift to yourself.

Materials Needed:

- 1 x Craft sized sheet of frosted shrink plastic

- 3 x 9mm Silver plated jump ring

- 3 x Silver plated key chain finding

- Assorted beads

- Silver plated head pins

1 Draw a picture onto a piece of paper of the sweet treats you would like to create. If you prefer, you can print an image out from the internet and trace over this. Use your shrink plastic ruler to gauge the size your treats will shrink to after you have heated them. If they are too small then just increase the size by drawing them slightly larger or enlarging them using a photocopier.

2 Trace the shapes of your sweet treats onto a piece of frosted shrink plastic with a pencil. Cut the shapes out using a pair of scissors. If you prefer you can have a sweet treat that is all one piece or you can layer the pieces like I have done with the strawberry and ice cream cone.

3 Use various coloured glitter gel pens to decorate your pieces. Use a single hole punch to cut a hole in your pieces wherever you would like to place a jump ring.

4 Shrink the pieces using a heat gun for a few seconds or by placing the pieces into an oven. Shrink according to the manufacturer's instructions and recommended temperatures.

5 If your pieces consist of layers that need to be stuck together, mix some two part resin glue and use a cocktail stick to apply this to component parts and stick them together. Hold the pieces in place for two minutes to allow the glue to dry a little. Allow the glue to dry completely for three hours.

6 Attach a jump ring to the hole you made in the piece before shrinking and attach a jump ring. Attach a key chain to the jump ring before closing it. Thread a head pin through a bead, create a loop and attach the head pin to the key chain. Wrap the wire around the base of the loop and trim off any excess wire. Repeat this process with the other beads and key chains.

RESOURCES

All of the materials and jewellery making tools and accessories I have used throughout this book were provided by the following stockists:

Silver Clay Creations

www.silverclaycreations.co.uk

- Shrink plastic products, jewellery making kits and accessories, jewellery making workshops, DVDs & books

Beads Direct

Unit 10, Duke Street
Loughborough LE11 1ED
Telephone: 01509 218028

www.beadsdirect.co.uk

- Shrink plastic products, shrink plastic jewellery making kits, beads, gemstones, Swarovski, findings, jewellery making accessories, flat backed crystals

Other useful resources:

David Airey Photography

david@silverclaycreations.co.uk

- Jewellery & product photography, jewellery photography master classes

Victoria & Albert Museum

Cromwell Road
London SW7 2RL

http://www.vam.ac.uk/page/j/jewellery-and-adornment-learning-resource/

- One of the finest and most comprehensive collections of jewellery in the world. Over 3,000 jewels at the museum and lots of learning resources and inspiration on the V&A website.

Natalia's other jewellery making DVDs and books are also available now at www.silverclaycreations.co.uk

Templates

Fossil

Heart

Skull

Large flower

Medium flower

Small flower

Rounded flower

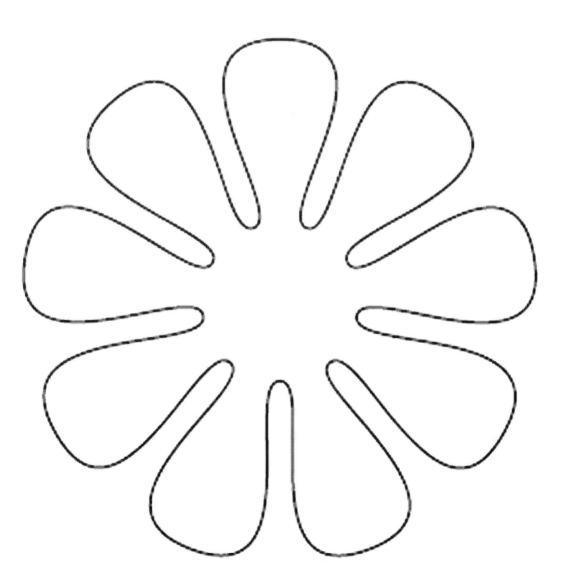

Peacock brooch

Hummingbird

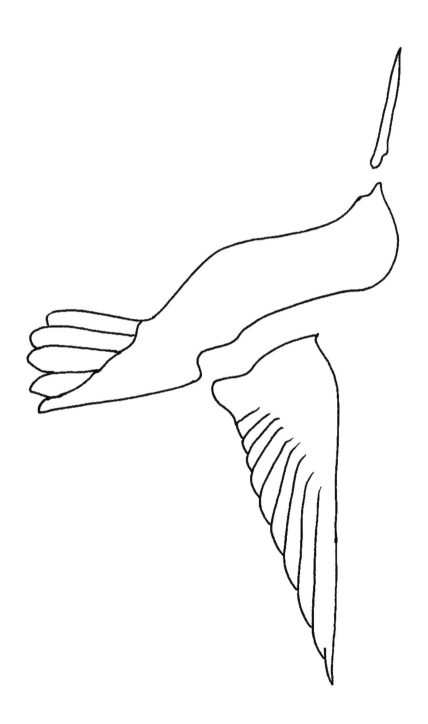

Owl necklace

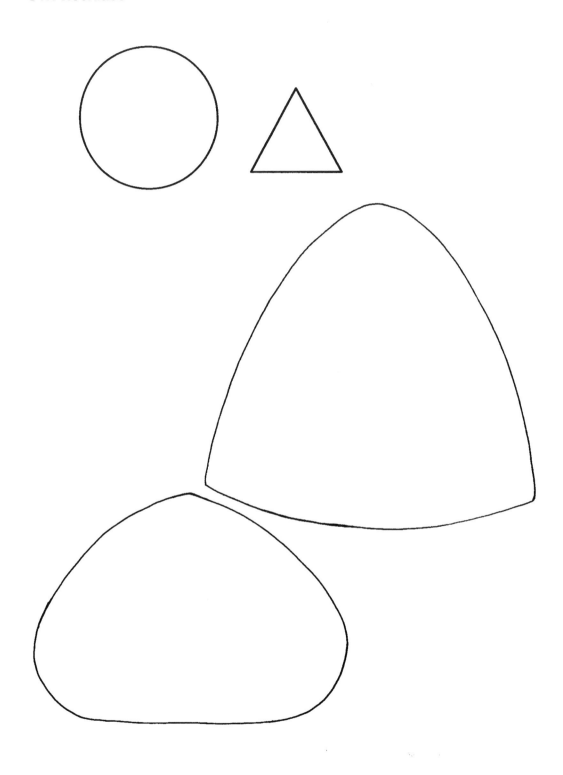

Gingerbread man

Gingerbread women

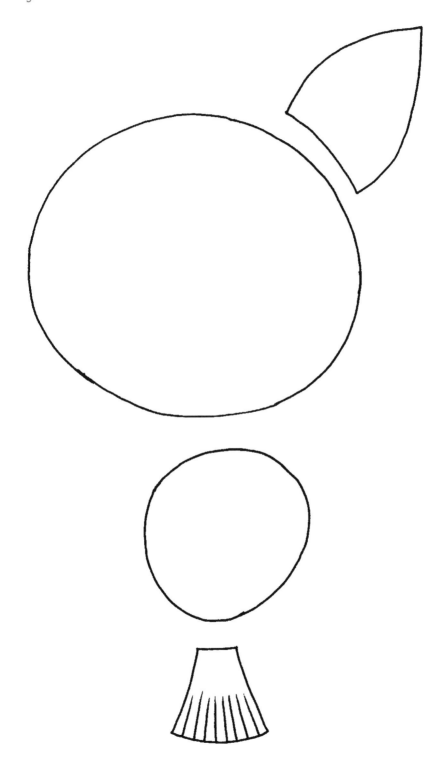

Cupcake

INDEX